Across Countries of Anywhere

Across Countries
of Anywhere

Pauline Hanson

alfred a. knopf   new york   1971

to Mother

and to Wallace

contents

Across Countries of Anywhere

The
Forever Young
And
Never Free

with the young and dead of other wars

———————

the many

What we must come to in now this deepening dread,
we still deny, we still would leave unsaid.
The fatherhood is mortal and of hate;
the only brotherhood is of the dead.

And the ferment—must the ferment in us
still work its slow, its quickening way between us?
Or somehow, somewhere, sometime will it stop
and love begin that has not yet begun?

Young—you cry to us for your lives; but what
you ask us to remember, we forget.
You cry against your death; but we have wept
and the emotion has not found its thought.

Our lives as we live them so order your death:
never known to us or soon to be forgotten—
with the young and dead of other wars
in your dying, your unlived lives are wasted.

When we who grieve for you no longer grieve
and these many memories of you thin and give,
who will remember that the dead have died
for what the infatuate living will not live.

To ourselves our words whisper every waste.
And now our hands—not lifting to their grace—
put down their monstrous shadows until again,
again these ceremonies are of hate.

This evil that in its rituals still shrives
itself of death and death again—this evil
so moves upon the young that these even
before they die in it have lost their lives.

We in ourselves, if we would sometime see
how this thing was and is and is to be,
will somewhere, past emotion into thought,
see the forever young and never free.

Variables in the constant, each who dies
dies in the ethic lie and practised phrase.
And again this end and this beginning
are moments of what the living will not change.

In a world our own lives will not change,
first our selfishness and then our hate
hide us from ourselves and from each other.
And this is what your death perpetuates.

But while this time of death once more defines
the timeless enmity of man and man—
hating and hated, which one of us can say
"The secret will of evil was never mine."

Men speak good words yet none they speak atone
the secrets of the selfish flesh and bone;
nor can I listen but with deepening dread
in years that search their goodness and my own.

In the greatest and in the least of us,
the moral consciousness, never at rest,
compounds the elements of an oppression
in which we are oppressor and oppressed.

Our own minds make us creatures of the oppression
that asks of us a derelict submission.
If it will, let thought be passionate—
but let it be thought and not be passion.

In what forgotten days were these begun?
And what was lost in them and what was won
that who dies here, that who dies now, cries every
goodness gone and every death undone?

What good can ever take its rise from force
that lives with pity but without remorse.
Yet where can goodness come from but from us
who wait for it and will not be its source.

Remorse that we should feel we have not felt;
and though your young lives again are spilt
to the imperatives of our desire—
we turn from truth, for truth must hold our guilt.

As in nightmare, now the circle centers:
until in shadows, until in sudden faces
that take and terribly become our own,
must we not know our fear is of ourselves?

Again, again the end brings the beginning.
And in this last which is this first reckoning,
so simple is the answer, now each mind
must make the question the impossible thing.

We move to what we want until it comes
that each at last moves in the stratagems
of the "good" who have not lived their goodness
and the "wise" who cannot live their wisdom.

The mind is flesh—and selfish for ourselves
we still, by every stealth of selfishness,
would refuse the moment of knowledge because
how can we know and now forgive ourselves.

But if we sometime would not turn from it
then how greatly would we learn from it
that this moment, like the moment of love,
has other lives, has all of life, to give.

This is hope and all the hope there is:
that sometime in knowledge and the wish of it
one will say, alone and with forbearance:
"Love begins as I begin to live it."

The moment waits on us and passes—and
as even now the old realities
must come from our not changing evil: tomorrow
comes from yesterday and from today.

Ourselves the evil and the only good
each who fails himself is well afraid.
For in the question in the answer, each
is mortally his own immortal God.

Begotten of our selfishness and grown
to our complexities of hate, now in
the gathering in against ourselves we only
know how deathfully life bears its own.

The old, too old for death, live in the lie
in which too young for their death, the young must die.
But sometimes between this and another dying:
dead—there are words the speechless try.

The living keep the lie; the dead, the truth—
and if we listen: in again their anguish
the dead repeat the relentless ways in which
the psychic orders the somatic death.

with the young and dead of other wars

_____

the one of love

When this is done and in its time is quiet,
slowly, and then in its mortality,
the body goes from life to death of life
or goes from mystery to mystery.

Not in the way the day goes into the night
and we remember it; never in this way—
but as the known goes into the unknown
and the finite into the infinite.

The mind dreams to its death and in its anguish,
waiting, and in all its wish to live,
it takes life from the dark earth of the body
until the body has no life to give.

When its death runs where its life once ran,
and these are not two things but only one,
the mind at last returned into itself
is the body and the body's pain.

If we dream into our own darkness,
if we sleep and wait in our own quiet,
if sometime we have another consciousness—
always the mystery is of the flesh.

The bloodbeats keep their own chronology;
they stop the century and stop the day.
And breaking, stop the thought it is by them
that we take time from its eternity.

So the living body must submit
its life of feeling and its life of thought.
So it must find itself and lose itself—
and what was finite becomes the infinite.

You said—and always the words were their torment:
"Men make their many Gods and live in them
until, too dark to see against the darkness,
every God is one and he is death."

"And the relentless earth is flesh of him
and all of time is his immortal breath. . . ."
And this—was this the way it was for you
when torment left the words? And when words went?

Of such as we—begot, not yet begot—
ever again some think what some cannot:
that who will lose their fear in faith will forever
keep to themselves this consciousness, this body.

I cannot say of you what these have said,
nor leave you, as they leave you, the epic dead.
The long lie whispering into now the truth
tells your death and tells your death wasted.

In the indifferent dust men sleep the same
for each who goes to it gives it his name,
humbled by the opposeless pain that thus
returns him to the earth from which he came.

This first year has a not explained beauty
and what it means—how slow I am to see.
Until one day the yellowwood is flowered
but flowered to show me your mortality.

The thought comes, still, that this is beauty drawn
from the winter of its year, whereupon
the hope I had reckons the doubt I have
that we put off the cerements we put on.

You said: "The flowered earth is loveliest
to those who know themselves the dispossessed."
Though that was in another year, today
you die again in all that you have lost.

You die again—and with your dying sight
now I see how infinite the night is
and how the morning is a mist on the fields
and how the flowers there are made of light.

Or now I see with all your grief of sight
the moment of a small bird's crimson flight.
And because I live and now you die in it
such a moment sings the first and last of time.

But now your sleep is mine and I dream down.
And in the earth where death is never done
what is there for the dead—do the dead dream
from flesh to dust, from dust to resurrection?

Life would reason death another way
but reason will not come or will not stay.
Or what thought is there to think when from his death
a lover speaks what dead men cannot say.

In a questioning that is a long
and not perceptible abandoning,
you are everywhere, yet you are nowhere;
you are everything, yet you are nothing.

The heart that breaks to say your obsequies
will ask its ease of you—will ask its ease
and will break again to learn how poor a thing
love is if love is less than what love was.

Sometimes, remembering, I come again
to the foreverafter of the dream.
And as I believe, I believe again
in birth and death and only love between.

But in love that is not love enough, I let
the years lie upon you like a winding sheet
that covers now your life and now your death
and I—if I remember, I forget.

When love becomes the memory of love;
when grief I had is all the grief I have;
when the shadow has at last no substance,
I will have done what I will not forgive.

The while, in my too little love, my own
lifts in his granite face the burialstone
of the young who even as I forget them
are the forgotten and the never known.

In the many, the one of love turns far
and always farther into their despair.
But if his voice is love, is death, is silence,
always he tells me how alone the dead are.

In the giving up and the letting go,
in the quiet earth's eternity,
unprovided and afraid I come
to what I would and what I would not know.

1948
1957
1971

From Creature
to Ghost

———————

Across the night
until beside me,
the wild dogs crouch
and the hunted, the hurt thing,
cries its anguish,
begs its life.
But night is a country
of dying and dead
and when night voices howl
somewhere and how
the body is torn—
shuddering out of it

what small thing is this
so slant, so uncertain,
the moon will not show
nor darkness describe
the slow way it moves

from creature to ghost
and now from the home of
its body is lost.

Is lost, is alone,
yet so great this anguish
of dying and dead,
I think the small ones
of all the earth
sometime are met in it.

Or time is always
of once and now.
And in any night
when the wind is black
and the wild dogs leap—
hunted and tormented
and torn from the body,
like the animal ones
of all the earth
I come to everywhere,
everywhere this darkness.
And shuddering into it

if once I was only
the one who listened
listening has made me
the one who cries.
Until in this place
of dying and dead:
from creature to ghost
the way is so strange—
I die, I live,
in the anguish of both.

And
I Am Old
to Know

————

No place seemed farther than your death
but when I went there—gone from there,
it was from your love you spoke
and it was to your love I moved.

And as you speak it—you, my own:
in the days, in the nights of your voice,
always the word of love opens,
opens into all its meaning.

And as I longer move to you,
as you wait and as you take me,
not like a lover but like love
you tell me and I am old to know:

love is to the farthest place—
love is to so far a place
from always its greater distances,
to see where death was, I look back.

The Ways

In the fields of evening where
another April held the crystal
of now not day, of now not night:
I saw, who looked with April sight,
that where the yellow legend flowers
folded the yellow legend in,
the way was in the luminous spring
and then in the remembering.

Where the constant winter was,
where stricken from myself I went
into the cold and colder sweep
of snow on snow already deep:
where once waiting and white the way
was to the everywhere of winter,
was where I found and could not keep
the wish of winter and of sleep.

And once, beyond the words of it,
slowly then all suddenly,
imagined in the longest night
the way, the only way, was time.
And with more wonder than my own
such understanding came—to find
the way across, I sang it: but this
was when the body was its spirit.

When you touched me, when I touched you,
when your shadows, when my shadows,
shimmered into the sensuous flesh
of my body, of your body:
lust into lust we moved and then—
then dreamed from every secret self
of our remembering, it was
like lost . . . like found . . . like always love.

When pain took flesh, took bone, took breath—
when in its raging knowledge my body
dying, dying, was not dead,
what was I and what was it said:
to the body pain gives back
pain rages. Or now in words of death
pain whispers to explain the despair
of which I must but can make no prayer.

And was a stranger of myself
and went into the other world
into the mysteries of madness
until so sweet it seemed no madness

until so sweet it seemed the sweetest
the sanities of every sense
and other words that said still say
this inward is this outward way.

Ourselves the never to be known:
does something of us sometimes dream
into out there . . . into out here . . .
another place? From there . . . from here . . .
one with what dreams in us, we dream
to yesterday and to tomorrow.
But never of our knowledge know
the way we come, the way we go.

So Beautiful
Is the Tree
of Night

When I see how high it is,
when I see how its great branches arch across the sky
and how from there, all of a blackness,
its branches bend over and down
until down to the world that must lie in its shadows—
when I see this,
so beautiful is the tree of night,
in country and in country
I am whoever watches it.

And when in their long flight to somewhere,
small and shining birds
begin to come into its darkness;
when its great branches are heavy with them—
heavy with the ones who find their quiet sleep,
heavy with the others who in their dreams of flying
shake their silver feathers—
when I see this,
so beautiful is the tree of night,
before the day fades it
I watch from century and from century.

Love

———

Of your lives and of your love
you gave, I took. And remembering how it was
I know you knew in all the years
of what you gave and what I took from you,
as who was young I never found you.

But now: if sometimes I only know the anguish of
too late this love that grows in me and reaches out
and you not here to take it—
is it how I think my way
to you who have the names of now the dead,

from your lives is how love comes to me.
And as it grows in me—
the way through me love reaches out to others:
am I old to learn it,
this love is yours and is the way I find you.

one with the dead

In the forever of the flesh
I forget.
        But I remember.
Until I know the way—is this
the way the dead move from their bodies
from their now other bodies
that cry, that cry to who will hear them:
"Will you from our love take love
and from our lives take life and always
always from our death take death?"

Vast in the night, these other ones
my own and dead, touch me to shadow.
Until as I am one of them,
in now the darkness of for us
this reaching back, this reaching out—
dreaming to the ones I love,
dreaming to them, dreamed to them,
are these words mine, their words whisper:
"Life is, death is, for us this waiting."

And in the night, the quiet night,
because I cannot stand alone
before the mystery of myself:
waiting in what waits for me—
here and from another place,
now and from another time,
the dead put out their darker hands . . .
but I have hands as dark, as dark.

Stars

---

i

When the first stars

come into the gray
air of evening;

when their sudden bodies
follow each other into the night
and everywhere cling to its walls;

when everywhere, against those black walls,
their bright bodies move a little, or their wings beat the air—
then, and even when driftnets of cloud gather them in,
their flight is like the flight of moths.

For if I wait, not a driftnet of cloud
but the wind has fingers to tear it: and lovely to see
how from every height of above me
the remembered bodies of
stars like moths tremble out.

Now the dark waters of the night

deepen upon the world,
deepen upon it and cover it.

And in the faint light that comes down,
if I watch how the slow stars float
above houses that have the curious shapes of coral;

if I watch the slow way stars gather
between the frondlike branches of tall trees,
and the quick way they scatter when with each cold
sweep of these waters, the trees shake them out;

if I watch how some stars rise
to where the surface waters break and are white now with foam,
I wait; and before their bodies again glitter through:
in always the cold wash of these waters,
I think them small silver fish.

iii

However I turn from them,

these are the vast altars of the night
and on them, the stars are candles set for the dead.

And when I think it
and we who have stood and will stand here
know it is only as shadows of each other that we come and go;

when I think it
and from time that was and is and will be,
our voices in requiems of wind
ask our questions and refuse us the answers;

before these timeless altars of the night,
all in a darkness in which bodies cannot hold us in:
not to try the mystery but to celebrate it
we move in this how strange,
in this how common, act of worship.

iv

Written across the dark pages of the night,

the stars are words,
and we look up at them.

To try to understand what they write, we look at them
until not from these moments
but from these years of our lives:

if we read them into belief,
if we read them into unbelief,
the sentences are so large
what is small is lost from them.

Nor can we remember when it first was:
read into belief, read into unbelief—
one had the sound of the other. And this?
this is because we grow old and old
and begin to understand what they write.

To see what it is

is to see how in a million years of this darkness
a star struggles from dust to luminescence;

is to see how afterwards it shines by consuming itself,
is to see how it ages then, and how it dies
and is itself the dust from which stars are born.

And to see through telescopes more than a billion
and beyond telescopes and beyond numbers, yet more
of these blazing worlds of gas—to see them
in the terrible atomic winds spin and spiral and spill

white, violet, purple, bloodred, and out
out into black, is to think: and in everywhere
the movement and flow of always that energy,
our own bodies have their breath, have their sight and thought
and have this slow until this sudden wish of words.

That Other
Silence

---

i

I think it.

And from the years of my life,
from more lives than my own, it gathers.

I think it. And it gathers.
But not into sound. And in the silence around it
the thought, whatever it was, is lost.

And yet from that silence: always the wish
is to speak,
is to speak to each other,
is to know ourselves spoken.

And for this—in the ordinary of my days,
in the insistent nights of my body,
whatever my wonder,
whatever my torment or my terror,
what I want—

in oracles of listening, what we want
is to try it in words.
For to try it in words
is to think it into sound,
and to think it into sound
is to remember it into knowledge.

Is to remember it until slowly, suddenly,
in oracles of listening we move in, we live in—
yes, an answer: but an answer lost
in everywhere the question of that other silence
out of which? into which?
with words, we try to think our way.

ii
_____

Across the winter of a day,

in ritual garments as white as of snow the trees,
like men of sacred orders, bend to their prayers.

And they pray me to follow and I follow them
until in a place hidden and haunted and away, they put out
the black bones of their fingers, their arms, and above me their faces.

Or with a thrust of green, of yellow, of crimson,
here, in the spring of a day, the first flowers come up.
And as quick and as rich—up from another darkness,
underwords come. And the undersong rises.

Or up from the sunbright field where I wait:
to show me the summer of a day—in each upward leap,
in all the long fugues of their flying,
these purple martins, now alone, now together,
repeat it. And repeat it.

Until above me, as if in a book lifted
and held there by the hands of time,
a colder morning opens its pages of light.
And across those pages, in black and delicate sentences of flight
the bodies of birds write, that I may remember
and from them may sing, what begins, what is gone.

And in the ordinary of my days,
if what I remember has only the sound
of why, of how, of when, of where:
in oracles of listening
a small word becomes a world
as large as I can know it.

iii

I dream but this, in the night, is the way I wake.

I go out—out into silence beyond silence
but out there, silence is the way I listen.

As now: I never spoke the words; for not speaking them,
   something of me yet sleeps.
But in this heavy fragrance of the linden trees: to listen
   is to remember . . .
until I wake into, until I move in, a world not spoken too late.

Or now as they rise on the nightdark river, now as they walk on its waters:
out there, those bodies? from our different places in the dream
we listen to each other, we speak to each other—
if I wake into, if you wake into, these white figures of mist.

Or now in these changing, these tormented degrees of consciousness:
above me, high above me, out there, out here, the hands of time meet
and I wake in everywhere by those dark hands set free
the stars are like small birds flying and I want—
what I want is to write them, is to write myself, never away.

But when oracles of listening bring them
down and words tremble through—to take them
is to remember the outstretched hands of the dead,
is to remember the outstretched hands of the not born.
And as I wait, as I wake: in this silence of the spirit,
slowly, suddenly, the hands I put out are not mine.

And if everywhere from each other and from ourselves
our bodies, like figures of mist, fall away;
if now from our lives, if now from our death, we take for our footfall
the slow sound of the rain—a little farther out, a little longer—
knowing ourselves taken by them we listen to each other,
we speak to each other: from the earth, the air, the waters.

_iv_

I grow older

and I live in the ordinary
of more than my own days.

I grow older
and I live in the nights, insistent, now,
of more than my own body.

And whatever my torment
that the going on
is never to the comfort of the answer
but until it is death is into a question;

whatever my torment of it,
whatever my terror—
I am only answered
as I remember, as I move in,
always the greater mystery of the question.

For in oracles of listening
revelation is as often
as the answer there is no answer
shatters into the sound and drifts with the echoes
and is lost and begins again in the silences
of why, of how, of when, of where.

And as often as I remember it from the years of my life,
and remember it from more lives than my own:
with a fullness of terror which slowly, suddenly, is ecstasy—
I move, I know we move until death and afterwards,
in the sound, in the echoes, in the silences,
of a question larger, always larger than it was.

We Meet

---

i   before me, after me

Drank my way.

Was as if of every way to not alone
the most mysterious was to drink it?

Went as far as . . . I thought but more than I thought I drank—
this talking together . . . this closeness
might this be where? might this be when?

Out as far as but our whiskey wisdoms came to such confusions
. . . and if the voices, if all the voices were my own—
no, it was only to myselves I went,
was only as far as to myselves and was not far enough to go.

Until out as far . . . as far as to a world . . . in the darkness of
helpless in it, was as if in mysteries never to be understood . . .
was as if in profundities of understanding nothing, nothing,
drank into a world . . . for myselves and yourselves and the others,
together in it . . . was where was when . . . out into a largeness of

out into an ecstasy of . . . felt for each other a kind of love
until as far, was far enough to find but never to be lived in
if hands never more than almost touch,
if words never more than almost speak,
together was like alone and the largeness, the ecstasy, how slowly it
was, is, between us, only these drunken distances. . . .

Or staring into them—to go as far as I can go, I return to: look.
On the wall . . . in a mirror . . . deep enough into it
and into my own aloneness is the way to not alone?
Because myselves as they come back to me bring with them the others
and while every mystery glitters into the not mystery of it—
with the ones whose eyes will not leave mine:

look they tell me and across the distances of time, look I tell them
is it pink and pig that imagined itself profoundly perplexed?
is it stuporous? and degraded? that out there was ecstatic?
More miserable than mystic, here is a face, stares at a face—
before me, after me, is this not anyone . . .
staring into, staring out from, anyone's eyes?

_____

ii all in the wanting to understand

And this? All in the wanting to understand it—

listen to it and sometimes into what it is
music sings us and is why we meet.

Or trying to write it into words, trying to read it from words—
as it rises into the sound of someone else's,
as it rises into the sound of my own wanting to understand it—

across countries of anywhere,
with centuries of death between us,
as ourselves but not as only ourselves, we think to each other—
we think to each other and in this we meet.

Or against space of space more vast—far from us, nearer to us,
here with his Chinese brush and ink, one of us drew these flowering
    branches.
And into the infinite whiteness of what is beyond them—
if something of us wants to go over, wants to go out—
are they to hold us back . . . are they to let us through . . .

drawn as we are from bodies so small
the smallest drop of ink would be too large to show us,
drawn from who we are into what we are—
of what we are to ourselves and to each other,
of what we are, of what we are meant to be,
here there is nothing, nothing our physical eyes can see.

Until in a picture about whoever looks at it—
one with who drew it, one with the ones now as then drawn into it,
our absence becomes a visible absence, becomes so invisible a presence—
with before us what only at first seems to be an emptiness of space:
drawn into more than our own not being here,
drawn into everywhere the not understanding it:

the wanting, the struggling, this is to come to what in ourselves
    is so pure—
in moments in which we infinitely give ourselves to it—
one with what out here is nameless, is formless,
how can we speak it? or show it? This experience of, this is to return to:
the stillness of it, the whiteness of it,
is of the spirit moving into . . . moving out from . . . itself.

iii   not in another time, not in another place

So monstrous the things done to them—

was it a year or a thousand years ago—
not dead, never dead, the way it was is how they come to us.

As there are nights when in every heightened pitch of wind
they scream from then to now the agonies of not their dead but of
oh God! their bodies racked . . . burned . . . broken. . . .

Not dead, never dead. Nor is it only in the night they come to us.
For up into the brightness of the morning—up goes a small brown thrush
and in a day of our indifference, we come upon them as suddenly
as above us, higher than we can touch him, the child hangs.

And this one! Oh God! Hanged here, another prison camp Jew—
the father, the mother—of their own heaviness, around them
the air would have a large, would have an awful violence on it
and on that violence, in that violence, they could struggle
to their death and from then to now would not so slowly die.

But so small and starved that of his own weight he cannot die!
This one? Oh God who for these hours is to let him hang here—
with his hands tied, with his feet tied—put here for the others to look at—
put up here as high as he has seen at home branches hang and
he reached up his hand but could not touch the flowers on them,
could not touch the shining apples on them;

put up here—if up here he sleeps away from how they did it . . .
if he sleeps into at home the boy down there—
from down there, only the boy looks up at him . . .
and he remembers but up up until he remembers into again
his neck, his head, his eyes. . . . And now he wakes in—
not in another time, not in another place,

again up here—in the monstrous endless agonies of it
now he wakes in, hangs in, is this cutting burning choking. . . .
And when his face swollen and black begs us why?
When from the questionmark of his small body he terribly,
terribly and always more clearly questions us into it—
in a total goodness not God enough to take him down is where we meet.

iv   so vast the door

I thought to be alone.

But so vast the door,
so strange the dark sweep of it,

to let me in
it opens from here and from there,
it opens from now and from then.

Until from everywhere the gray streets of the day,
from everywhere into these black aisles of the night,
you . . . and one by one the others . . .
come after me . . . or came before me.

And if I cannot see
the face you lift, the hands you put out;
if I cannot touch you, if I am never to tell you:
with my sight, with your sight, I see how the great stars burn
not to lighten the darkness but to show it.

And for the living who now from their death come to this place,
for the dead who yet from their lives return to it:
above us, around us, white figures of cloud
so quietly rise on the darkness . . . and move to each other,
gather to each other, all in so midnight an anguish of
their changing, their wraithlike, their own lost bodies . . .

as I think it with your thought, as you think it with mine,
across the countries, across the centuries,
of our eyes lifted, our hands held out:
are we the ones remembered, forgotten, never to be named,
are we the ones gone, the ones not yet come,
our shadows as they pass, pass into each other.

Until with the ones who wait in these black aisles of the night,
with the ones who walk in again these gray streets of the day,
as ourselves but not as only ourselves
we move into an understanding of . . . we move in the mysteries of . . .
how mortal the living, how immortal the dead.
There, here, then, now.

Questions
of The
One Question

The stuff of the world is mind-stuff.
A. S. Eddington

part one

—————

i

In bodies as many as the moments of time,
of what seems to come and go
yet in its passing
is what passes into always itself—
across these centuries of wanting to know what it is
have I named it Brahman?
or named it Tao?
have I called it God-Nature?
or called it the One And All?
Across these thousands of years:
thinking of it as Existence? as Life?
am I now to reason it as Mass-Energy?
Whatever the mystery of it
—always a part of it,
never apart from it,
what it is is what I am.

As however small it is,
the part is part of what is infinite—
more than a life, more than a separate life—
what I am is what Life is.

But Life? *What* Life is?
That what Life is is more than I can understand . . .
this means . . .
. . . what I am is more, is infinitely more
than my now consciousness of what I am?

If flesh is matter,
if flesh, as matter is,
is a special state of energy?

Passing from one to another
moment of time? point of being?
are the changes all strange changes
in degrees? in intensities?
of animation? of awareness?
In everywhere the flow of it:
of what it is, of what I am,
has there ever been—
how can there ever be—
a not being?

———————

ii

Who I am?
If who I am had a face.
If who I am could look at who I am.
If who I am could be looked at . . . or be looked for . . .
or could anywhere be found.
If who I am were flesh and as flesh
could touch itself or touch another of its kind.
If who I am could think about itself . . .
and could itself speak and listen to the words:
"This who I am? who am I?"

But my body—if my body is to question itself—
spoken, listened to,
the question isn't: "This who I am—who am I?"
The question must be: "What is who I am?"
Until: "This what I am—what is it?"

For if what I am imagines itself
into such a word as who:
imagined but not created—
who I am doesn't exist.

iii

Of what is infinite—an infinite self
is what my imagined finite selves most dread.
But if in its wrong thinking,
my body thinks it loves my body?
The within? the without?
one repeats because one is the other.
And if not in nouns but in verbs,
what I am begins to question what I am?
The form does not love, does not hate, the form:
remembering that what it is it cannot itself understand—
flowing through the form
what loves or hates itself is the transforming power.

Subject always, but a changing subject:
the ones I was before I was born?
At the moment of birth—that one?
And afterward—moment by moment
the ones of the first years? the ones of the last years?

Strangers to each other . . .
each the total of an awareness
never before exactly experienced—
what each in its passing felt, thought, was,
left it a body—as that body,
gone now, how can it ever again be lived in?

But this aging one? the one I am at midnight?
Like the others
an aging body has only itself to question.

But the blurring outlines of an aging body?
If in its now midnight awareness
its outlines blur into the blurring outlines
of behind me, of before me,
other bodies . . . other forms ? . . .
If these at midnight are the blurring outlines of what I am. . . .

As morning comes,
as my midnight body ages into this morning body—
aware of gone now but all of them lived in,
aware of waiting for me but how can I imagine them:
what I think of, what I feel—these blurring outlines?
these are the outlines of
for me, even for me, an infinite being?

Wanting to know what it was—
this, I said, is the basic unit of the universe?
But did I think of this smallest part as the particle
never to be penetrated? never to be divided?
Not solid, not substantial—the atom is porous?
And smaller than this not smallest part:
what are its orbiting electrons?
and the mass-energy of its nucleus . . .
vibrating in this mindlike part . . .
vibrating into a halo of what so vastly waits to create? to destroy?
To name what I can't know is not to know it.
But now—and with its positive and negative charges
is the atom now a particle? or a wave?
—dividing it, always dividing the not known into the not known:
what are its protons? its neutrons? its mesons? its positrons?
 its neutrinos?
And its muons? its pions? what are these?
Orbiting, transmuting into each other—named but not known
all are particles of? waves or vortices of?

Is the not known ever to be divided into suddenly the known?
What I search is an atom—but an atom of what?

The stuff? the structure?
built up by its atoms, the universe is the unit.
And if not knowing what it is,
I think of the universe as space for, time for,
one, only one vortex of everywhere always
energy into matter, matter into energy?
In the great circle of things in the process of being created . . .
in a circle in which a beginning reaches back, reaches out,
    into always a beginning. . . .
Is the secret more easily to be found in the smallest part?

I think of an atom and I think:
with its positive and negative charges,
with its vortices, its energies—
in what is everywhere an always transforming flow
an atom is an electrical system?
a series of events? a transformer of power?

And my body?
If as a man of science, I think of my body's 10^{28} open and
    almost empty atoms:
except for the mass of the protons and electrons of its atoms—
my body is an emptiness of space?
collect "me" into such mass as my body has—
I am a speck of something
too small to be seen unless with a magnifying glass?
That body? Or familiar to me—this body?
But as I come to know my not knowing,
even as the body familiar to me—what am I?
As my body was growing,

atoms here since the beginning of time were being added to it
until now—built up by now my 10^{28} atoms?
Living on an earth bombarded by a rain of cosmic radiation,
pierced as I am by a never-ending barrage of atomic particles—
in my body there are every second
the explosions of a thousand nuclear fissions?
Only sustained by the atoms
of the oxygen I yet breathe and of the food I yet consume:
am I the changing experience of
every second in my body a thousand nuclear fissions?
Built up by my atoms . . . existing as
myself a series of events? myself a transformer of power?
in what is an always transforming flow—this is what I am?
an always changing total
of positive and negative . . . constructive and destructive
energies?

---

v

If I think of the universe as an exploding mass?
If I think of whirling away from the common center of it
its billions of fragments—
each fragment a galaxy of hundreds of billions of stars?

If I think of only one of its fragments—this one, in which
    the earth exists?
. . . a spiral galaxy of 200 billion stars?
world-large fiery globes? spinning? fissioning? exploding?
all of them flung across space of such remoteness
the darkness of a billion miles separates the nearest of any two of them?
Until I think of the earth, I never come to a vastness I can imagine.
But if I think of its place in a spiral galaxy of 200 billion stars?
suns of such whirling size and fire—
among them, our sun is only a common kind of star . . .
only a pinpoint of light?

On the orbiting globe of an earth
a million times smaller than the small sun nearest it . . .
I try to think of the whole and of the parts and I think. . . .

Disks, globes, spheres, spirals, vortices. . . .
The atom? and its nucleus?
In a halo around the nucleus, its electrons?
The larger circles of orbiting around the sun,
the earth and the other planets?
The sun circling out through this spiral galaxy?
The not to be imagined vastness of this galaxy—its smallness lost in
beyond it, the spiral nebulae?
And out . . . out from the spiral nebulae? . . .

Disks, globes, spheres, spirals, vortices—
the pattern in how many ways shows itself.
Born in the circle of new bodies created from old bodies:
I think of the parts? the phallus? moving into the vagina?
I think of the mystery of suddenly the egg-sperm cell?
of how it develops into the sphere of the blastula?
until from that hollow sphere there develops
the three-layered germinal disk of a human body?
finding in the round of the womb? the foetal position?

Remembering—to make them, the rounds of my fingers;
to see them, the rounds of my eyes;
I think of: even the sundial? the hourglass? the compass? the clock?
the wheel for the cart? the telescope? the microscope?
And I think of: so magic it encompasses the globe of the earth,
magic enough to explore the universe—the circle of the zero?
And if I remember the way in which blindfolded I go out
only to come back? back to the beginning? . . .
Remembering other not to be broken circles—
I think of the serpent with its tail in its mouth?
and the wheel of existence?
And I think:
matter and its energies? flesh and its desires?

in the timeless circle of fission, growth by assimilation until fission again,
born of what I am—what am I?

In the never to be broken circle of the question:
sometimes . . . almost understanding. . . .
I look at the halo around the head of a saint
and remembering the flow of everywhere what energy is . . .
remembering it as vortices of what waits to create or destroy—
I think: in the flow of what it is, from any life
this is the way its goodness circles out? . . .

Or its evil?
In a beginning—was the universe
the cosmic explosion of its atoms?
The creation of its own destruction—
is the universe space for, time for,
one, only one vortex of everywhere always
energy into matter? matter into energy?
Born of a cosmic fissioning—
at once self-destroying, self-creating and again self-destroying:
through such matter, such flesh,
always the impulse to fission?

And my body? on a globe as insignificant as the earth?
If I think of out from this gathering evil . . .
out from . . . out into . . . circles of
now its larger its more terrible violences?
In the flow of what it is
and on as small a bit of stone and metal as the earth—
everywhere its reaches. . . .
And I think: built up by my atoms,
with its atoms, slowly quickly
is my body to destroy the body of the earth? I imagine:
the fiery surges of fissioning atoms

the demonic tongues of blazing gas
the churning clouds of glowing vapors—
reaching everywhere everywhere up and out
out into earth-encompassing tornadoes of fire, of radiation. . . .

But if I think of stars millions of times larger than the earth?
and the vast blazing violences in which those giant globes
so massively relieve themselves by fission? by explosion?

For a bit of stone and metal a million times smaller
than the pinpoint light of the small sun nearest it—
for so insignificant an earth? so briefly vaporized?
how is size to be fixed? or time?

In the night of my not knowing, I look out—out
until in the dark remoteness of galactic space . . .
I think

engulfed by it, absorbed into it, one with it,
I am . . . the earth is . . .
the stuff, the structure—built up by its atoms, the universe is the unit.
In a timeless circle of forms created from forms destroyed:
moving as if with love and hate for what it is—
everywhere the movements of, changes in, its forces.
Everywhere its always transforming flow.

---

vi

Matter and its energies?
flesh and its desires?
born of what I am—what am I?
In a not to be broken circle—
one with what it questions
the question as it shows, is the structure.
And as it whispers it, is the stuff.

In the vortex of my wanting to know:
I must think—three billion years to make me,
is the secret in whatever it is
the energy of this wanting? this thinking?
If my body thinks of itself not as a particle but as a wave—
thinking not in nouns but in verbs,
through my body what it is explains: this wanting?
in the circle of forms being created from forms being destroyed,
to exist is to want, is always to want
a never attained perfection of not wanting.

As in any beginning—
the question fissions into fissioning questions without number.
But scattered as they are across space, across time:
is any one of them a world
large enough to live in? to be lost in?
questions of the one question,
in the vortex of my not knowing,
the vortices of my wanting
are only different moments of the search.

To search the secret of three billion years to make me:
of what makes me, I make my microscopes, my telescopes.
And is the secret more easily to be found in the smallest part?
Is it the atom I search?
or with now electronic microscopes, cyclotrons, bevatrons,
I search—smaller than the atom—the vortices within it?
Searching in the atom these mysteriously
appearing and disappearing vortices of wanting—
part transmuting into part,
question transmuting into question:

"I" am a body built up by its atoms? by their transmitting power,
staring into this instrument I search this atom
until as what I am, what I am must think
in the atom, in my body, this wanting this searching—here
here whatever it is
is the mystery of what searches itself?

And continuous with
now in the nucleus of this atom, its vortices—
continuous with now in this thought
a nucleus of this energy to think it. . . .
Out from these smallest vortices—

up from out from wherever they are,
my bodies as they search through my microscopes and telescopes
and my bodies as they want and write these words. . . .
Vortexing out from the insignificant globe of the earth—
continuous with up there the galactic violences
of atoms and electrons blazing across, sprayed across,
space of a remoteness of a darkness
continuous with, forever continuous with

itself the energy of any concept of itself
is it the universe it questions? or the atom?

Searched for through instruments less to be marvelled at
than in my body the searching instrument of my brain—

as phantom as this moment of this searching it,
the mystery is of something
as mysterious as in flesh
the first unrest of the question.

part two

Is it what feels itself as here now "my" senses—
is it here now what thinks itself to be "my" mind—
of a mysterious something
as much outside as inside me,
what is it?

If my body
is the way the mystery sometimes questions itself,
if what it is, if what I am,
is energy wanting to know what energy is?

To know what I am as what is infinite—
this is to know myself fulfilled.

Or to be endured as then, as now, the smallness of my thought:
at this ancient burial place,
inhaling . . . exhaling . . . one of the atoms of oxygen
he—how many centuries ago—inhaled . . . exhaled?
Here, in the thought of once a Chinese emperor:

did I think that when I died
I could keep my sacred person
seven times beyond the hands of Death?
Did I think that I would be and men could put here
not what I am, but only who I was?
With everywhere the earth the air the waters:
around me, Life has its awesome ways
of reaching down and up . . . of reaching in and out. . . .
But are its hands to take me:
here, in a seven-fold coffin . . .
what I am must seven times longer wait?

Or close to this ancient burial place:
less sacred than an emperor—if I think of my body
as put in a five-fold coffin? as put in a three-fold coffin?

Or not there but here—to be endured as again
and again the smallness of my thought:
for what I am I made a world no larger than
a world as small as—
here on the sands of a desert—this pyramid?
or now . . . on a shelf—this urn?
On an earth bombarded by a rain of cosmic radiation—
in a never-ending barrage of atomic particles,
stone is a flesh of atoms so easily pierced . . .
in the flow of what everywhere moves
though here it moves as a darkness a silence of waiting:
in the moment of these hundreds of these thousands of years—
for what I am in a pyramid? for what I am in an urn?
is Life a strangeness of . . .
or less or more than this
is Life an animation of . . . an awareness of . . .
something kept out that wants to come in?
something kept in that wants out?

If my body
is the way the mystery sometimes questions itself—
"my" body?
if action is everywhere the interaction of atoms? . .
if bodies take the forms their atoms give them? . . .

Not to be imprisoned
by any shell of stone, of wood, of ego:
if I think of not there, not then, but here now
released to the earth of the burning grounds,
in the smoke rising into the air,
in the ashes cast on the waters—
the "indestructible" atoms of what I was, of what I am,
    of what I am yet to be?

And if I think of other ways
in which the humble more easily inherit
the earth the air the waters?

As when vultures have gorged themselves on my flesh. . . .
The heavy hideousness of up from their feeding?
The excrement thick on trees where they hugely roost?
of that excrement—the scattering dust?
. . . of that dust—the elements?
taken by the earth the air the waters?
This? Is this what I am?
. . . yet in their bodies—the heat of vultures mating?
And the watching—through all these slow circles of flight
the now ravenous watching? Until this black scuttling down
. . . and again . . . on the Tower of Silence:
flesh of how many of them—
this hunger, this gorging? . . . Is this what I am?

―――――――

viii

If what it is, if what I am,
is energy wanting to know what energy is?

For creatures of the earth, of the air, of the waters;
for trees, flowers, grass;
or of the least of these—even for the smallest seed:
whatever its form, for itself each is flesh . . .
is flesh and in its own way is aware . . .
is flesh and in its own way, wants. . . .

What in flesh gathers to intensities
of awareness, of wanting. . . .
Everywhere. Everywhere real.

But is it anywhere to realize itself?

If it gathers . . . until as in humankind
the wanting is a wanting to know. . . .
if wanting to know what it is,

it yet more strangely, yet more wonderfully gathers—
gathers until to the greater intensity of words. . . .
If it comes to its greatest intensity
when the sound of its wanting to know itself
is the sound, is the experience, of its own not knowing. . . .

For humankind: this, isn't this the only way
it can realize itself?
when embodied in flesh
it can speak to itself and can listen to itself . . .
but whether it speaks and listens to itself
in questions or in answers—
in the words of one as in the words of the other,
it knows itself the never to be known?

ix

In the vortex of my not knowing—
when what I am so gathers that
here now I am this poem is these vortices of wanting to know?

This wanting—are words the sound of it?
does it in words express itself? celebrate itself?
—until never explaining what it is
WORDS ARE THE EXPERIENCE OF

WHAT THE MYSTERY IS—
HOW CAN THE MYSTERY TELL ITSELF?

Has it in me named itself Brahman?
or named itself Tao?
Has it in me called itself God-Nature?
or called itself the One And All?
Across these thousands of years:
thinking of itself as Existence? as Life?
does it in me now reason itself as Mass-Energy?
Naming itself, yet only to be known as the not known:
with its imagined and changing truths about itself
does it in me question itself
into before its beginning, into after its end?

In the movement of, changes in,
what is everywhere a presence:
in a beginning reaching back reaching out into
    always a beginning,
to be what it is is more than to know what it is.

Itself the energy of any concept of itself:
if what it is is what it is doing . . . .
If what it is
is doing it doesn't know what. . . .
If the mystery of *what* it is
is the mystery *that* it is. . . .
In bodies as many as the moments of time,
subject always, but a changing subject—
do I say I search it?
it has said in me it searches itself.

What it is it cannot itself understand.
But *that* it is?
To be what can be for itself
a sweetness of the senses?
a miracle of mind?
To be what knows itself an infinite mystery?
To be for a moment of time the terror, the ecstasy of it?

A mysterious something
aware of itself as awareness . . .
a mysterious something in its flow
self-creating, self-destroying and again self-creating . . .
search it searching itself:
inside me outside me
crazed? celestial? demonic? divine?
the mystery is of something continuous
with the first unrest
of what must question itself.

A Note on the Type

This book was set on the Linotype in Bodoni Book, so called after Giambattista Bodoni (1740–1813), son of a printer of Piedmont. After gaining experience and fame as superintendent of the Press of the Propaganda in Rome, Bodoni became in 1768 the head of the ducal printing house at Parma, which he soon made the foremost of its kind in Europe. His Manuale Tipografico, *completed by his widow in 1818, contains 279 pages of specimens of types, including alphabets of about thirty languages. His editions of Greek, Latin, Italian, and French classics are celebrated for their typography. In type designing he was an innovator, making his new faces rounder, wider, and lighter, with greater openness and delicacy.*

This book was composed, printed, and bound by H. Wolff Book Manufacturing Co., Inc., New York. Typography and binding design by Betty Anderson.